WHAT LEADERS SAY ABOUT THE BIBLE COMPANION

The Bible Companion's creative and relevant insights will shift your daily Scripture study from a "have to" to a "want to." *The Bible Companion*'s invitation to experience one chapter of Scripture per day helps you fall in love with God's unfolding story and empowers you for everyday faith.

—Kara Powell, chief of leadership formation at Fuller Theological Seminary
Executive director of the Fuller Youth Institute Coauthor of *Future-Focused Church*

The Bible Companion is well named. Like a friend who loves the Bible from cover to cover, this series will stay by you as you read all sixty-six books as one story. The books will give you fresh insights on familiar passages as well as help you discern the stories embedded in those hard-to-read books like Numbers and Ezekiel. If you want to see the Bible with fresh eyes, this is for you.

—Janice Cunningham Rogers, founder of Youth With A Mission School of Writing
Author of *Is That Really You, God?*

Karen Moderow's insights and the easy-to-follow format will help us to establish rhythms of Scripture engagement that will take us to depths we long to go but haven't had a path to take us there. *The Bible Companion* is a trusted friend that will accompany us on our journey to understanding the very heart of God through Scripture, revealing His love and purposes for us.

—Dr. Beverly Upton Williams, CEO of Haggai International

When the church is open to the Holy Spirit and God's Word, we will see the greatest awakening in history (Hab. 2:14). As pastors and leaders, we need *The Bible Companion* like never before to help eradicate biblical illiteracy. This series helps believers see the panorama of God's story with His special creation—us.

—Loren Cunningham, founder of Youth With A Mission International
Cofounder of the global University of the Nations

Christian people want and need the Bible to become their book. That is an exciting, if daunting, challenge. *The Bible Companion* offers just the accompaniment many readers need. It is a wonderful resource that walks with Bible readers as they make their way through either the whole or parts of the Bible. By all means, take up its offer, then walk in the light of God's Word.

—Mark Labberton, president of Fuller Theological Seminary (Ret.)

The Bible Companion is a great resource for leaders looking to energize their own daily Bible study or to strengthen teams by studying God's Word together. Short daily readings with thoughtful applications make this series doable even with a busy schedule.

—Brad Lomenick, founder of BLINC
Author of *H3 Leadership* and *The Catalyst Leader*

WHAT READERS SAY

Never have I been so captivated by the integration of big-picture patterns with the fine details of the Bible's stories as with *The Bible Companion*. Karen Moderow's approach is bold, realistic, and truth seeking. *The Bible Companion* is a fantastic resource for first-time readers or for those ready for a deeper-level study.

—Michael Pavlisin, founder of Impact Through Awareness

Growing up as a Christian, I'd read parts of the Bible, but reading the Bible all the way through seemed very intimidating. Daily readings in *The Bible Companion* help to break down the chapters one by one, in digestible bite-sized pieces. It highlights the main points, explains the key takeaways, and provides relatable guidance that I can apply to my own life. This series has made me excited to read more and learn more. It's reinvigorated my relationship with God and provided a great opportunity to share the experience with friends and loved ones. It's a beautiful feeling to grow closer to God again. Thank you, *Bible Companion*!

—Armine Kourouyan, senior project manager for USC Hollywood, Health & Society

Karen Moderow's beautifully and intelligently crafted Bible series revolutionized my personal devotions. I've read the Bible through but was looking for fresh insights and help understanding difficult books such as Leviticus. *The Bible Companion* walked me through parts of Scripture I had stumbled through before. The series helped me see a loving, invested God woven throughout Scripture from the first page to the last. *The Bible Companion* has given me a greater love for the Word of God. I wholeheartedly recommend it.

—Blossom Turner, Christian fiction author

THE BIBLE COMPANION

BOOK 5

JOB

JOB
Journey through Scripture One Day at a Time

THE BIBLE COMPANION

BOOK 5

GOD IN POETRY
BOOKS OF WISDOM

KAREN WESTBROOK MODEROW

JORDANWEST

© 2025 by Karen Moderow. All rights reserved.

Published by Jordanwest Publications.

Noncommercial interests may reproduce portions of this book without the express written permission of the author, provided the text does not exceed five hundred words. When reproducing text from this book, include the following credit line: Karen Westbrook Moderow, *The Bible Companion Book 5 Job* (Dana Point, CA: Jordanwest Publications, 2025).

Commercial interests: No part of this publication may be reproduced in any form, used to train generative AI in any form, stored in a retrieval system, or transmitted in any form by any means—electronic, photocopy, recording, or otherwise—without prior written permission of the publisher/author, except as provided by United States of America copyright law.

Artwork by Kristine Brookshire.

Unless otherwise indicated, all Scripture quotations are from the Holy Bible, New International Version®, NIV®. Copyright © 1973, 1978, 1984, 2011 by Biblica, Inc.™ Used by permission of Zondervan. All rights reserved worldwide. www.zondervan.com. The "NIV" and "New International Version" are trademarks registered in the United States Patent and Trademark Office by Biblica, Inc.™

Scripture quotations marked (KJV) are taken from the King James Version, public domain.

Scripture quotations marked (MSG) are taken from THE MESSAGE, copyright © 1993, 2002, 2018 by Eugene H. Peterson. Used by permission of NavPress, represented by Tyndale House Publishers. All rights reserved.

Scripture quotations marked (NCV) are taken from the New Century Version. Copyright 2005 by Thomas Nelson. Used by permission. All rights reserved.

Scripture quotations marked (NKJV) are taken from the New King James Version®. Copyright © 1982 by Thomas Nelson. Used by permission. All rights reserved.

Scripture quotations marked (NLT) are taken from the Holy Bible, New Living Translation, copyright ©1996, 2004, 2015 by Tyndale House Foundation. Used by permission of Tyndale House Publishers, Carol Stream, Illinois 60188. All rights reserved.

ISBN 978-1-963080-31-5 (Paperback)

978-1-963080-09-4 (ePub)

DEDICATION

For my father, Pastor Floyd Westbrook,

who wrote the early versions of this series,

whose love for the Lord drew me to Christ, and

whose passion for God's Word inspired the faith of many.

THE BIBLE COMPANION SERIES

SET 1	GOD IN BEGINNINGS	BOOKS OF LAW
	Book 1	Genesis, Exodus
	Book 2	Leviticus, Numbers, Deuteronomy
SET 2	GOD IN STORY	BOOKS OF HISTORY
	Book 3	Joshua, Judges, Ruth, 1 & 2 Samuel
	Book 4	1 & 2 Kings, 1 & 2 Chronicles, Ezra, Nehemiah, Esther
SET 3	GOD IN POETRY	BOOKS OF WISDOM
	Book 5	Job
	Book 6	Psalms
	Book 7	Proverbs, Ecclesiastes, Song of Songs
SET 4	GOD IN WARNINGS	BOOKS OF THE PROPHETS
	Book 8	Isaiah, Jeremiah, Lamentations, Ezekiel, Daniel
	Book 9	Hosea, Joel, Amos, Obadiah, Jonah, Micah, Nahum, Habakkuk, Zephaniah, Haggai, Zechariah, Malachi
SET 5	GOD IN JESUS	THE NEW TESTAMENT
	Book 10	Matthew, Mark, Luke, John
	Book 11	Acts, Romans, 1 & 2 Corinthians, Galatians, Ephesians, Philippians
	Book 12	Colossians, 1 & 2 Thessalonians, 1 & 2 Timothy, Titus, Philemon, Hebrews, James, 1 & 2 Peter, 1, 2, & 3 John, Jude, Revelation

TABLE OF CONTENTS

From the Author 13

How to Use This Book.. 15

The Bible: What Kind of a Book?...................................... 17

The Books of Poetry 19

The Book of Job... 21

      Job 23

      The Structure of Job... 28

Resources 83

      Forty Significant People of the Bible 84

      Small Group Guide.. 86

      90-Minute Study Guide.. 87

Endnotes 88

Acknowledgments... 91

FROM THE AUTHOR

LET'S BE HONEST—THE BIBLE CAN be daunting. It's a big book. Some parts confuse us. Other parts (dare we say it?) can be boring. We also love to reread our favorite passages. But that verse from 2 Timothy nags at us—"*All* Scripture is given by inspiration of God, and is profitable for doctrine, for reproof, for correction, for instruction in righteousness" (2 Tim. 3:16 NKJV, emphasis added). We want to know what God says, but too often our good intentions fail when we reach Leviticus. If we're going to read the Bible all the way through, most of us need encouragement to make it through the hard parts. We also need accountability to establish the habit of Bible reading. *The Bible Companion* helps with both.

The Bible is a story. It starts with creation (Genesis) and ends with God rescuing men and women from a fight-to-the-death battle between good and evil (Revelation). How God ultimately redeems and transforms His creation opens our eyes to who God is. It also reveals who we are. A drama of love, betrayal, failure, and victory comes to life in the pages of Scripture.

There are many ways to read the Bible, but reading it from beginning to end connects us to God's bigger story. In Scripture, God reveals His plan for His creation through stories that build on one another. *The Bible Companion* keeps the story thread visible as you move from one book to another. The insights for each chapter pull you back into God's Word day after day.

As the Holy Spirit brings God's story to life, you'll find Bible reading a life-altering journey. There's no reading schedule. No checklist. If you miss a day, just pick up where you left off. The journey will be richer if you take a friend, your family, or a small group with you. The goal is doable. Small portions, every day.

Even if you've tried reading through the Bible before, try again. You're not alone this time. We can do it together.

Karen Westbrook Moderow

HOW TO USE THIS BOOK

THIS BOOK IS DESIGNED TO give you freedom to explore Scripture in ways that best suit you. The series is not a commentary or a devotional, though it has some elements of both—it's a companion. We will walk through the Bible together, asking the Holy Spirit to be our guide.

Read the Scripture first. Pay attention to how you react to the text—good, bad, or indifferent. Listen for any insights God gives you about what you read or what you feel. Then turn to The Bible Companion. You may want to use the book in one of these ways:

- Personal Journal: Record your spiritual journey.
- Legacy Journal: Make notes with future generations in mind.
- Family Journal: Read with the family and have one or more of you write or draw something related to the chapter on each page. You can sign and date entries to create a family record.
- Creative Meditation: Doodle, use sticker art, or paint to creatively "own" each chapter.
- Bible Study: Underline and make notes of truths you want to study more deeply.
- Respite: Enjoy the white space. Let an uncluttered page remind you to breathe and take in what you've been reading.

THE BIBLE: WHAT KIND OF A BOOK?

THE BIBLE HAS SIXTY-SIX BOOKS that tell God's story. Over centuries, more than forty authors inspired by the Holy Spirit wrote about God and His unfailing love for us using historical narrative, stories, poetry, letters, dreams, visions, and many other forms. Does the type of writing matter? We don't think about it, but anytime we pick up a book, we interpret what we read based on the kind of book it is.[1]

Take this example of the first line of a story: "The woman squeezed through the door and crept into the darkened room where the child slept." If we are reading a mystery, we may suspect some sort of crime is about to occur. If the book is a parenting guide, we may assume the woman is a mother taking care not to wake her child. However, if we are reading a book on child psychology, another interpretation becomes possible. We might view the scene from the perspective of the child, who, if awakened, might be frightened.[2]

In the Bible, genre—the kind of book or passage we are studying—gives us a lens through which to read. Genre facilitates the message, telling us *who* and *what* is important. For example, histories highlight people and events, whereas the law focuses on God's standards. Genre also sets expectations.[3] We shouldn't expect the laws on animal sacrifice to have the same devotional impact as a poetic book like Psalms. Nor should we expect Psalms to have the time and place details we find in historical books like 1 and 2 Kings.

Different kinds of writing in the Bible allow us to experience God's truth from a variety of perspectives. Some types will appeal to us more than others. What attracts us may not draw someone else. Scripture's many genres assure that each of us will hear God's message in a way that resonates. Personal preference doesn't exempt us from reading all of God's Word, but paying attention to the type of passage we are reading can help us find value in every text.

It's a mistake to think that the parts of the Bible we find difficult are less inspired, have less truth, or are less relevant. While much of the Bible contains clear instruction, God also inspired men to write Scripture in ways that make us wonder. God's Word often raises questions that require us to engage with Him and each other. This interaction is what makes the Bible exciting.

For help in exploring some of the creative ways God shares His truth, look for the short *How To* sections throughout the series. You'll find suggestions on how to read different genres such as the genealogies, the law, poetry, and end-time (apocalyptic) dreams and visions.

The psalmist prays, "Open my eyes that I may see wonderful things in your law" (Ps. 119:18). If we ask, the Holy Spirit will unlock some truth in everything we read. "For the word of God is alive and active. Sharper than any double-edged sword, it penetrates even to dividing soul and spirit, joints and marrow; it judges the thoughts and attitudes of the heart" (Heb. 4:12).

THE BOOKS OF POETRY

Wisdom Literature

POETRY IS FOUND IN ALL but a few books of the Bible.[4] In the Old Testament, poetry celebrates Israel's exodus from Egypt, announces that Hannah and Mary will have sons, and mourns the destruction of Jerusalem. In the New Testament, poetry praises God as Lord of all at the end of the world.[5] Five books in the Bible are almost entirely poetry—Job, Psalms, Proverbs, Ecclesiastes, and Song of Songs (also known as Song of Solomon).

We may wonder why God would inspire people to write of Him in poetry—a genre that depends on interpretation. Poetry is not an efficient way of communicating information. For that, prose is better.[6] But poetry tells us something important about God: He wants to engage not only our minds but also our emotions. Our Creator cares about the whole person.

In the books of the law and history (Genesis–Esther), God has spoken to us primarily through our universal love of story. In the poetic books, He speaks to our hearts. Poetry appeals to emotions, which may overwhelm us in times of great joy and sorrow. In joy, it gives us a language for gratitude. In sorrow, poetry connects us to God and others. Pain often shuts us down. Wounded, we care little for the arguments of philosophy or theology. We need to know someone cares. God speaks to us in poetry—the language of the heart—to assure us we are not alone. His presence comforts us as we battle life's hardships.

The poetic books are often referred to as "wisdom literature" because they make wisdom the foundation for thriving. Proverbs 9:10 says, "The fear of the Lord is the beginning of wisdom." Wisdom literature teaches us to live in ways that honor God, ourselves, and others. These books do not gloss over the harsh realities of life but guide us through them. Each book offers a perspective to help us find meaning and peace in life.

- **Job** teaches us that God alone is wise.
- **Psalms** teaches us how to worship.
- **Proverbs** teaches us how to live.
- **Ecclesiastes** teaches us to set priorities.
- **Song of Songs** teaches us how to love.

We don't approach these poetic books the same way we would the books of the law or the historical books. Poetry floods us with images that spark our imaginations. The truth they hold is not found in literal interpretations but in what the images symbolize. For example, in Psalm 23, we're not being asked to believe God is literally a shepherd but that He cares for us as a shepherd cares for his sheep. When the psalmists say God is their rock, their shield, and their fortress, they mean He is their stability, strength, and protection.

The adage "a picture is worth a thousand words" explains the power of poetry in Scripture. One image opens a whole world to us, a world where God joins us as we face the triumphs and heartbreaks of life.

THE BOOK OF
JOB

THE STORY OF JOB TAKES place in the land of Uz, far from Abraham and long before the Jewish nation exists. Its setting is the oldest in Scripture. Job's wealth is measured in livestock, as we would expect in an ancient tribal system. However, much of the book's action takes place in what resembles a Persian court. This tells us Job might have been written much later about a man who lived in an earlier time.[7]

Many scholars believe a Jewish sage exiled in Babylon used the story of this righteous man to anchor discussions about how God works in our world. Sages in the ancient Near East often gathered disciples who debated aspects of life.[8] Job reflects the Israelite perspective that there is one God who is all powerful and all wise.[9] Given this, the debate most likely takes place before a Jewish audience, though some theologians claim a rogue scholar uses Job's story to challenge the retribution theology common in his day.[10] Retribution theology claims people get what they deserve. The author questions this, along with other traditional views of wisdom offered by Job and his friends. The twist is that many of the axioms the book challenges come from Scripture, yet this questioning is divinely inspired. When we cannot reconcile the losses in our lives with the promises of God, God invites us to grapple with Him over what we don't understand.

For centuries the book of Job has been a source of not only comfort but also consternation for people seeking answers for why evil runs rampant in our world. But the book refuses to bend to our expectations. While Job provides insight into suffering, the book is not a defense of God. It gives no explanation for evil. In short, the issues we bring to the table when reading Job are not necessarily the ones the book addresses. Viewing the book only through the lens of suffering may block us from seeing other important truths essential to maintaining hope in a hostile world. The consuming question of the book of Job is not *why do the godly suffer*, but *who is wise?*

Ancient cultures revered wisdom. Modern readers find this obsession hard to understand, but Job will reveal wisdom as a key to surviving in a hostile world. We listen not because of any abstract theological argument

Job offers but because he rejects platitudes that we, too, may find insufficient. Job does this beautifully and poetically, but he's not nice about it. We like that. He raises argument to an art form. We like that too.

The book of Job is one of the great literary masterpieces of the world. The fact that Job is poetry tells us its unknown author seeks to engage us at heart level. We will find plenty of theological gristle to chew on, but pain, a constant companion throughout the book, tethers us to reality.

Theologically, Job has been billed as the biblical balance to the book of Proverbs.[11] Job exemplifies why we must base our beliefs on the whole of Scripture. Taken alone, Proverbs (as well as many of the "blessing and curses" passages of the Torah) had been misconstrued to promote a "retribution gospel."[12] Job refutes this theology—suffering does not equal sinfulness, and blessing does not always equate to righteousness.

God graciously allows us to take Job's journey with him so that we, like him, may be transformed by the truth. Faulty theology leads to disappointment. Truth leads to hope and resides in the person of Jesus Christ, "the only wise God" (Rom. 16:27).

JOB

JOB IS A WEALTHY MAN who lives in the time of the patriarchs. He's not an Israelite. His homeland, Uz, is a pagan nation. But Job worships God faithfully within the structure and knowledge of his day. Outside of the book of Job, he is mentioned in two other books of the Bible: Ezekiel (14:14, 20) and James (5:11).[13]

Through no fault of his own, Job loses everything—his wealth, his family, and his health. As he seeks to understand why this has happened, his spiritual journey becomes a road map for suffering people of all times. Job is praised for his perseverance. Though often angry, confused, and discouraged, he never loses faith in God, and in the end, grace—not entitlement—reverses his plight.

Job demands answers from God, which he never receives. But he's given something far greater—an encounter with God that changes his understanding of God, himself, and the world.

Job 1
A RIGHTEOUS MAN

Have you considered my servant Job? There is no one on earth like him; he is blameless and upright, a man who fears God and shuns evil.
      Job 1:8

JOB'S STORY WAS LIKELY TOLD for hundreds of years before it was preserved in written form. In between a prologue and epilogue, Job battles personal demons, his wife, his friends, and ultimately the LORD as he struggles to understand why God has turned on him.

We watch, first as spectators sitting in the heavenly court with God and Satan (the accuser). But as the drama unfolds, we find ourselves being pulled into the vortex of Job's suffering. Soon we'll be on the ash heap with him scraping our wounds because we can't escape the obvious—if Job can lose everything, so can we.

The wager between God and Satan disturbs us. Would God allow a righteous man to suffer to satisfy a bet? That Job is a poetic book gives us insight. Perhaps the scene simply creates a legal setting where our assumptions of justice will be tried. To build a theology of God's character requires a broader view of Scripture. In fact, much of what we encounter in Job demands we consider the whole of the Bible.

The wager, like many aspects of Job, resists a simple explanation. The imagery holds truth—God is a royal sovereign, and the accuser will condemn us. But God's response is not to make us pawns but to send His Son. Romans 8:33–34 asks, "Who will bring any charge against those whom God has chosen? It is God who justifies. Who then is the one who condemns? No one. Christ Jesus who died—more than that, who was raised to life—is at the right hand of God and is also interceding for us."

COMPANION THOUGHT

Describe a time when you felt used by someone. When did you realize it? Do you think God uses people as pawns? Why or why not?

*Naked I came from my mother's womb,
and naked I will depart.
The Lord gave and the Lord has taken away;
may the name of the Lord be praised.*

JOB 1:21

Job 2
GOD ALLOWS JOB TO BE TESTED

Shall we accept good from God, and not trouble?
    Job 2:10

JOB KNOWS NOTHING ABOUT THE law or the blessings and curses of the covenant,. But the author (writing in a later time) does. For centuries God's people have been taught that obeying Yahweh—the God of Israel—is the way of life. Disobeying Him leads to death. These principles are true but have been misapplied. The Jews have made Proverbs law, creating a perversion of Scripture. Proverbs 16:3 says, "Commit to the Lord whatever you do, and he will establish your plans." They would take this verse to mean whatever they pray about will succeed. Job's question, "Shall we accept good from God, and not trouble?" gives us our first clue that we will be questioning such assumptions.

If obeying God always brings life and prosperity, then why would trouble be an issue? Job acknowledges a reality—all people, including good people, suffer. Pain is a part of the human experience. But does it come from God? Job doesn't attribute the suffering to God, but he recognizes that no one or nothing can harm us except that God allows it. This is the first of many difficult truths in the book. God is in control yet often does not intervene. Job's friends will help us grapple with what this means. They will also teach us about the impact of relationships in hard times.

As we journey through Job, we will resist the temptation to sidestep difficult truths with religious clichés. This is exactly what the book fights against. For now, we sit with Job and his companions, mourning the pain and devastation in our world. We grieve with men, women, and children everywhere who suffer. We grieve for ourselves. As fellow sufferers, we, like Job, can fall on our knees before God. Though quaking, we can worship and cling to a faith that the Bible assures us will hold in the storm. "'Because he loves me,' says the Lord, 'I will rescue him; I will protect him, for he acknowledges my name'" (Ps. 91:14).

COMPANION THOUGHT

Who is on trial, God or Job? Why? When you sit "among the ashes," what person do you tend to blame? What person do those around you blame?

Job 3
JOB'S FEAR BECOMES REALITY

What I feared has come upon me, what I dreaded has happened to me.
    Job 3:25

STRIPPED OF EVERYTHING, JOB CURSES the day he was born. His rant, though not directed at God, rails against all that God has created, including himself. God allows it. As readers, this may stop us. God neither rebukes nor condemns what comes very close to blasphemy. He has said all along that He wants a relationship with us—a real one where we can be honest about what we feel. This passage proves He means it. Even more, in Job's lament, awesome in its imagery and force, God gives us a gift—language to express our pain and frustration.

Job's admission that he has lived in fear lets us in on a secret. People of faith can be consumed by worry. Job fears for his children. Job 1:5 says, "When a period of feasting had run its course, Job would make arrangements for them to be purified. Early in the morning he would sacrifice a burnt offering for each of them, thinking, 'Perhaps my children have sinned and cursed God in their hearts.'" We surmise his children partied hard and didn't have the same regard for God as Job. It also seems Job's wealth creates anxiety for him. He says, "What I dreaded has happened to me" (v. 25). The more he has, the more he can lose. Job's confession tells us fear is an issue to track in his journey.

Pain breeds more questions than answers. Job asks, "Why is life given to a man whose way is hidden, whom God has hedged in?" (Job 3:23). In other words, why would God bring us into this world and not give us the wisdom to make sense of it? Recognizing we do not have the resources to handle life alone is the starting point of faith. We can exhaust ourselves trying, but Jesus says, "Come to me, all you who are weary and burdened, and I will give you rest" (Matt. 11:28).

COMPANION THOUGHT

What is your greatest fear? How do you try to protect yourself against it?

THE STRUCTURE OF JOB

An introduction and conclusion by an unnamed narrator bookend the conversations Job has with himself, others, and God.[14]

STRUCTURE	TYPE OF DISCOURSE	SPOKEN BY	REFERENCE
Introduction	Prologue	Narrator	Job 1–2
Speeches	Monologue	Job	Job 3
Speeches	Dialogue	Job and friends	Job 4–37
Speeches	Deologue	God	Job 38–42:6
Conclusion	Epilogue	Narrator	Job 42:7–17

Job 4
WHEN REALITY AND GOD'S WORD COLLIDE

Consider now: Who, being innocent, has ever perished? Where were the upright ever destroyed?
   Job 4:7

ELIPHAZ IS FROM TEMAN IN Edom, a kingdom known for its wisdom.[15] He and Job's other friends represent the finest thinkers of the ancient Near East. They believe that justice is a simple equation—good comes to the good and bad comes to the bad. A broken Job sits in front of Eliphaz as evidence this cannot be true. The innocent do perish, and the righteous are destroyed.

Job's friends have only Job's word that he is innocent. They don't believe him. However, as observers in the heavenly court, we've heard God Himself say that Job is blameless. So from the start, Job's friends hold a faulty assumption. If they're wrong about that, could they be wrong about other things? We're being set up to question everything. Job's friends trust human wisdom, which we call *tradition*. Yet the axioms of Proverbs will enfold some of these traditional views. It will be up to us to apply them in a way that God approves.

This puts believers in scary territory. We must consider what source of wisdom we can trust. The whole of Scripture teaches that our ideas of right and wrong can't be the standard. "There is no one who does good, not even one" (Ps. 14:3, Rom 3:12). Job shows us that all beliefs must conform to the wisdom of God, or they lead to wrong assumptions.

For now, we sit with Job, shout out our pain, and bear the judgment of others, knowing that Jesus too suffered unjustly. "But if you suffer for doing good and you endure it, this is commendable before God. To this you were called, because Christ suffered for you, leaving you an example, that you should follow in his steps" (1 Peter 2:20–21). Seasons of suffering may mean waiting for long periods of time without answers or relief. But we do not wait alone. Jesus is with us.

COMPANION THOUGHT

Who do you turn to for wise counsel? Why do you trust them? What is the source of their wisdom?

*Those who plow evil and
those who sow trouble reap it.*

JOB 4:8

Job 5
JOB'S "COMFORTERS"

We have examined this, and it is true. So hear it and apply it to yourself.
     Job 5:27

ELIPHAZ IS LIKELY THE ELDEST, as he speaks first. What Eliphaz says about God is true. Dare we disagree? God does perform miracles. He cares for the earth, protects the innocent, and stands for justice. But there's a problem: reality doesn't match this expectation.

Job's story is not just the plight of one man but of all believers, including God's people. The Jews reading this passage would struggle with the disconnect between God's promises and their circumstances. (By the time Job is written, they are no longer a kingdom but are under foreign rule.) Eliphaz's words bring to mind the blessings and curses in Leviticus 26. Didn't God promise blessing to those who obey Him and cursing on those who didn't? The author doesn't mention this dynamic directly—Job's story takes place before the law was given—but the idea undergirds every argument Job's friends make. The first wave of exiles who've returned to Jerusalem are asking the same question as Job: if God's promises are true, then why are we suffering?

As yet, we have no answer. Pain makes us deal with the uncomfortable fact that things are not as they should be. There is a moment on the cross when Jesus cries out, "My God, my God, why have you forsaken me?" (Matt. 27:46). Jesus knows of God's redemptive plan. He knows God is at work behind the scenes, and still, suffering overwhelms Him. He protests. He cries out. Just as we do.

If Christ cries out, what does this tell us? Times of suffering call for compassion, not platitudes. A withholding of judgment, not accusations. Listening, not preaching. When we or others suffer, moving too quickly to the promises of God (even though they are true) tempts us to discount the pain. Being told to just "trust God" may add guilt. The Bible says, "Mourn with those who mourn" (Rom. 12:15). A loving presence may be the only comfort a hurting person can receive.

COMPANION THOUGHT

What situation in your life that you expect to be "blessed" feels "cursed?" What do people say that helps? What hurts?

Blessed is the one whom God corrects;
so do not despise the discipline of the Almighty.
For he wounds, but he also binds up;
he injures, but his hands also heal.

JOB 5:17–18

Job 6
A LESSON ABOUT PEOPLE

My brothers are as undependable as intermittent streams . . . that stop flowing in the dry season.
   Job 6:15–17

THE WORDS OF ELIPHAZ SEND Job into despair. For years he's lived before them with integrity. Unlike leaders of other powerful tribes, he didn't extort protection money from them. When he was attacked by enemies, Job never asked his friends to contribute to the cost of defense (Job 6:22–23). They benefited from his generosity. His stability ensured theirs. But when he needs their support, they abandon him. Job crumbles beneath their criticism and condemnation.

Job's friends can't get past a faulty theology that equates suffering with sin. Job thought his friends would be loyal to him, no matter what. Now he realizes that whatever lies ahead, he faces it alone.

Job's plight reminds us of Jesus in Gethsemane. Christ asked His dearest friends to stay nearby as He agonized over the cross. They failed Him—falling asleep first, then running away (Matt. 26:36–56).

When hurting, we long for human touch. Being let down by loved ones can feel like betrayal. Sometimes unavoidable circumstances separate us from family and friends. But other times those we depend on may not understand. They may be busy. Or they just don't want to be involved. Then we must accept that those we love may be less than we want them to be. This adds to our pain, but Jesus, again, is our example.

Christ did not turn His back on those who abandoned Him but gave His life for them. While we love and appreciate friends, our faith must be in God. He will never abandon us. "Though my father and mother forsake me, the LORD will receive me" (Ps. 27:10).

COMPANION THOUGHT

Is there someone in your life who repeatedly lets you down? What are you hoping they will give you? What would happen if you no longer depended on them for it but still maintained the relationship?

Job 7

A SOBERING REALITY

My days are swifter than a weaver's shuttle, and they come to an end without hope.
    Job 7:6

JOB DRAGS US INTO THE darkness with images that are poetic and awful. Like a slave without hope, he longs for the shadows. Monsters torture him at night, and the day brings no relief. His body, a mass of scabs and worms, disgusts him. Then it hits him—he is a dying man (Job 7:8). At last Job addresses God directly. He believes he suffers because God has not forgiven his sins (v. 21). He rightly discerns that unless God forgives him, he's doomed. But we remember that God had declared Job blameless (Job 1:8). Though Job doesn't feel forgiven, he is.

When things go wrong, we may dredge up past sins to explain our circumstances. After all, if suffering is always the consequence of bad choices, then we have more control. The alternative—that we live in an unsafe world where bad things happen to the innocent—is terrifying. This leaves us scrambling for security.

The Bible offers it. We can know with certainty that Christ's death atones for our sins. "If we confess our sins, he is faithful and just and will forgive us our sins and purify us from all unrighteousness" (1 John 1:9). Forgiveness doesn't address the problem of suffering, but it takes self-blame off the table. It means God is not against us. If He is for us, there is hope.

In the laments of this book of Job, God journeys with us through the dark. We rant with Job, as we should. But then what? Our suffering forces us to ask, Why would God leave us in this place? Is there something we can't yet see? Does God know something we do not? We suspect there is. So we come to Him not understanding, perhaps angry, but at last ready to engage honestly.

COMPANION THOUGHT

Do you want God to pay more attention to you or leave you alone? Why?

Job 8
THE PERILS OF ANCIENT WISDOM

Ask the former generations and find out what their ancestors learned, for we were born only yesterday and know nothing.
    Job 8:8–9

ELIPHAZ ADDRESSED JOB WITH RESPECT, but Bildad does not. Bildad says Job's children got the death they deserved (Job 8:4). It's a low blow. Despite the difference in tone, both men make the same claim—God is just; therefore, if someone suffers, they deserve it. This perspective embodies *human* wisdom.

Bildad advises Job to seek the wisdom of former generations for answers to life's perplexing problems. On the surface this advice seems grounded. There is value in experience. But when the wisdom of *man* conflicts with the wisdom of *God*, a choice must be made. Tradition held that God rewards the good and punishes the evil. Bildad warns Job not to question this. To the Jewish sages in Babylon reading this book, the idea that a righteous person could suffer was seen as an assault on God. Over the years the sages had elevated the Proverbs to law, something not supported by Scripture. The author fights back with reality.

Job's pain causes him to renounce the platitudes of old he once believed himself. Suffering does this. It softens us. Humbles us. Calls us to repent of the times we've judged others. Suffering reveals that we don't know everything. We are not wise. When we claim to be, we put ourselves in the place of God. "For the foolishness of God is wiser than human wisdom, and the weakness of God is stronger than human strength" (1 Cor. 1:25).

COMPANION THOUGHT

What is the difference between confidence and arrogance? Which do you tend toward when discussing family matters? Politics? Religion? Sports? Would your family and friends agree?

For we were born only yesterday and know nothing, and our days on earth are but a shadow.

JOB 8:9

Job 9
LASHING OUT AT GOD

Even if I summoned him and he responded, I do not believe he would give me a hearing. He would crush me with a storm and multiply my wounds for no reason.
   Job 9:16–17

WHEN GOD DOES NOT VINDICATE him, Job feels God has forsaken him. He wants to confront his Creator but can't compete with an invisible, all-knowing, all-powerful God. Though Job's only option for survival is God's mercy, he accuses God of being capricious and vindictive. Job is in so much pain that he no longer cares if God strikes him dead. He'd rather die than live as he is, but he isn't going down without a fight.

Trouble and pain make us want to lash out. When justice fails and God does nothing, when the wicked are allowed to grow stronger, isn't an all-powerful God responsible? Job asks, "If it is not he, then who is it?" (Job 9:24). Men and women have asked this question through the ages. We want God to accept our premise that the innocent should always prosper and the wicked should suffer. When we chastise God for not running the world accordingly, God seldom responds.

His silence exacerbates our frustration, but at some point, despair can push us in another direction. Disillusionment can cause us to question long-held beliefs. It is then God dares us to let go of what is false and follow Him into a deeper understanding of Him and His ways. Holding to faith during such questioning requires strength beyond ourselves. We need God, but perhaps trouble has strained our relationship. Like Job we cry, "If only there were someone to mediate between us, someone to bring us together . . ." (Job 9:33). Job longs for the Mediator we know has come—His name is Jesus.

COMPANION THOUGHT

Describe a time when you were at an impasse in a relationship and someone else helped you get past it. What did they do?

*He performs wonders that cannot be fathomed,
miracles that cannot be counted.*

JOB 9:10

Job 10

DESPAIRING OF LIFE

I loathe my very life . . . Why then did you bring me out of the womb? I wish I had died before any eye saw me.
    Job 10:1, 18

FOR JOB, DEATH LOOMS AS "the place of no return . . . the land of gloom and deep shadow . . . the land of deepest night" (Job 10:21–22). He wishes he had never been born.

In Job's complaint, we see a pattern—glimmers of truth distorted by faulty beliefs. He acknowledges God's existence. He knows the LORD created him and controls the world. He admits God was good to him early in life but now believes His kindness was a subterfuge. The Creator plotted Job's misery all along. "But this is what you concealed in your heart, and I know that this was in your mind" (v. 13).

Job presumes to know what God thinks and what His motives are. In fairness, Job suffers in the dark. The depth of God's love for him through Christ has not yet been revealed. Jesus has not risen, so Job has no assurance of an afterlife. This life seems to be all there is. Convinced he's suffering because God targets him, Job begs God to leave him alone.

"God is love" (1 John 4:16). This truth may seem at odds with our circumstances, but the whole of Scripture begs us to be patient. The snapshot of our life at any given moment is not the whole picture. The Bible tells us there are realities we can't see. No matter how desperate our circumstances, God is working behind the scenes for our good. Joseph as a slave in Egypt, Esther as a young woman in a king's harem, or Ruth as a destitute widow could've imagined the future God had for them.[16] Their stories remind us that we don't know enough to make sense of our suffering. We are neither all wise nor all knowing. But God will prove Himself even as we accuse Him of hurting us. He allows us the comfort of lament. He even suffers our abuse. But He will not leave us. "Be strong and courageous. Do not be afraid or terrified because of them, for the LORD your God goes with you; he will never leave you nor forsake you" (Deut. 31:6).

COMPANION THOUGHT

Think of a time when you were doing what was best for someone even though they accused you of trying to hurt them. Why did you do it? Would you do it again?

*You gave me life and showed me kindness,
and in your providence watched over my spirit.*

JOB 10:12

Job 11

ZOPHAR SPEAKS AGAINST JOB

Oh, how I wish that God would speak, that he would open his lips against you.
    Job 11:5

JOB INSISTS THAT GOD HAS afflicted him knowing he was righteous. Zophar joins Eliphaz and Bildad in condemning Job's position. Zophar's wish that God would disclose the secrets of wisdom to Job brings us to the central issue of the book—who is wise? Is it Job, who claims God is unjust? Or Zophar, who insists Job is guilty? Both men speak some truth. Both men err. Zophar, representing the wisdom of the ancients, seems to have the edge. The sage asks a series of questions that are good questions but are insensitive and inappropriate in the context of Job's suffering.

Wisdom is not just knowledge—it's applying knowledge at the right time, in the right way.[17] Zophar fails in three ways. He is arrogant (insisting his view that God never allows the innocent to suffer is correct), he is judgmental, and he uses the truth to bludgeon a hurting man. Zophar, who suggests Job is as foolish as a young donkey, is the foolish one. He accuses Job of stubbornness and blindness, the very things of which Zophar is guilty.

The lessons of Job are not just for the suffering but for all of us who are tempted to judge another's pain. God's wisdom calls not only for truth but grace. It's wrong to speak true words if the intent is to hurt or put others in their place. It's unwise to speak true words at the wrong time. Jesus, The Word who became flesh, is "full of grace *and* truth" (John 1:14, emphasis added). Truth will have its day, but Christ, who embodies wisdom, calls us to also embrace the wounded with gentleness, kindness, and mercy.

COMPANION THOUGHT

Why do you think Zophar is so eager to reprimand Job? Why we are quick to criticize our friends?

Job 12

JOB REPLIES WITH SARCASM

Doubtless you are the only people who matter, and wisdom will die with you!
    Job 12:2

JOB CHALLENGES HIS FRIENDS' PRESUMPTIONS that they are wise. He too is well versed in theology and wonders how they can claim God runs the universe justly when anyone can see that thieves and blasphemers go unpunished. Even nature teaches that the strong survive. He concludes, "To God belong wisdom and power; counsel and understanding are his" (Job 12:13).

Does Job believe this? Do we? Perhaps in theory. But there's a difference between paying lip service to truth and living it. Testing reveals that gap.

We shouldn't overlook the role Job's friends play in this process of discovery. We despise their know-it-all attitudes. Their condescension. Their callousness toward Job's suffering. But they force Job to confront a hypocrisy in himself he's not been aware of before. As Job defends himself to his friends, he clarifies issues for himself and us.

In hard times, we pray for friends to support us. Sometimes God grants it, but other times he allows friends to disappoint, frustrate, and even antagonize us. And while we're tending our wounds, God asks us to see ourselves, our circumstances, and our friends through new eyes. The inconsistencies between what we say and what we believe become apparent. Then we must choose whether the words others speak to us in anger and judgment will destroy us or burn away what is false.

Criticism can reveal how much we've depended on others to define our faith. Job has spoken the truth—wisdom belongs to God. But the truth scares him, and it scares us. If God's wisdom does not protect us from all harm, can we trust it? Can we trust God?

Proverbs 3:5 says, "Trust in the Lord with all your heart and lean not on your own understanding." Our circumstances may be unfair, but God asks us to rely on His character. He is love and He is just. In time He will prove it.

COMPANION THOUGHT

Describe a time when you needed a friend but friends and family distanced themselves. Why did they do that? How did you get through the crisis?

*To God belong wisdom and power;
counsel and understanding are his.*

JOB 12:13

Job 13

THE BOTTOM LINE

Though he slay me, yet will I trust him.
    Job 13:15 KJV

JOB CRIES, "YOU ARE WORTHLESS physicians, all of you" (Job 13:4). His friends insist that justice prevails in this world, but Job turns the tables. He says their traditions pervert God's truth. In the New Testament, Jesus calls out the Pharisees for this same thing. "You have let go of the commands of God and are holding on to human traditions" (Mark 7:8). When we preach God's law but ignore its heart, we turn it into a tradition of man. Job says, "Your maxims are proverbs of ashes" (Job 13:12).

Backed into a corner, he takes a stand. Even if God takes his life, Job will trust him. His faith rests in a God he does not understand. Addressing the Lord directly in verse 21, he asks for relief from his suffering ("withdraw your hand far from me") and relief from his fear ("stop frightening me with your terrors"). He makes one more request—one that suffering people through the ages have longed for—the opportunity to question God (v. 22). Job goes in circles, repeating previous arguments, wondering if God's punishing him for past sins and suspecting God has targeted him. He prods God to answer one question: *Why?* Job raises this question over and over. God gives no answer.

God's silence adds to our pain and tests our faith. But like the father of the tormented son who prayed, "LORD, I believe; help my unbelief!" (Mark 9:24 NKJV), we may ask our heavenly Father to guard our faith as we wait for some sign that God hears and will answer. Until then the whole of Scripture tells us to trust His love and His wisdom. Ecclesiastes 3:11 says, "He has made everything beautiful in its time." In time God will redeem our suffering, even as He redeemed the suffering of His Son, Jesus. Despair is not the end of God's plan for us, but the beginning.

COMPANION THOUGHT

How does the wish list you had as a child compare to your wish list as an adult? If different, what accounts for the change? How do your prayers today differ from those you prayed years ago?

*Though he slay me,
yet will I trust him.*

JOB 13:15 KJV

Job 14

A SERIOUS QUESTION

If someone dies, will they live again?
    Job 14:14

IN ANCIENT TIMES, LITTLE WAS known of life beyond the grave. People believed either that life ended at death or that as the body decayed, it was consigned to a sub-existence in hades. Hades was thought to be a place of shadows and gloom, horror and hopelessness.[18] The grave meant the end of meaningful life. Job says, "At least there is hope for a tree: if it is cut down it will sprout again. . . . But man dies and is laid low; he breathes his last and is no more" (Job 14:7, 10).

Job's mind tells him death is the end, but his spirit tells him there must be more. Tortured in body and soul, he cries out, "If a man dies, will he live again?" The writer of Ecclesiastes tells us God "has set eternity in the human heart" (Eccl. 3:11). We've been created with a longing for immortality and an awareness that life exists beyond what is visible in this world. But we had no basis for believing . . . until Jesus.

Jesus's resurrection breaks the power of the grave and frees us from fear of death. We know what Job does not—those who hope in Jesus follow Christ into a transformed, eternal life. "The body that is sown is perishable, it is raised imperishable; it is sown in dishonor, it is raised in glory; it is sown in weakness, it is raised in power" (1 Cor. 15:42–43). To the believer, Job's question is not a longing but a bold exclamation.

COMPANION THOUGHT

Is believing in life after death easy or hard for you? Why? What do you think you will do in eternity? How do you feel about it?

*Surely then you will count my steps
but not keep track of my sin.*

JOB 14:16

Job 15

WISDOM WITHOUT MERCY

Listen to me and I will explain to you; let me tell you what I have seen.
    Job 15:17

ELIPHAZ STARTS OFF THE SECOND round of the debate with accusations. He claims Job's own words condemn him. His refusal to admit his guilt undermines the beliefs of God-fearing people. Eliphaz asks Job if he has a monopoly on wisdom. In case Job has forgotten he stands alone, the sage reminds him that "the gray-haired and the aged are on our side" (Job 15:10). Eliphaz means that in rejecting his counsel, Job rejects God (v. 8). We bristle at his arrogance, yet the picture Eliphaz paints of an unbeliever's life rings true. Isn't there wisdom in living with integrity as the tradition of the ancients teaches? Is God behind what Eliphaz claims or not?

All wisdom originates with God and was evident in the world long before the Bible was written. For centuries sages observed that choices mattered. They collected sayings that distilled moral principles into memorable phrases to help people choose wisely. God inspires the authors of Psalms, Proverbs, Ecclesiastes, and Song of Songs to embrace these principles, called proverbs, in their writings. But they come with a caveat: the wisdom of God is built on the fear of the LORD (Prov. 9:10).

Without the context of a relationship with God, a set of moral laws will either crush us or make us arrogant. They become the tradition of men. Grace, a key attribute of God's wisdom, requires we apply the law with compassion, discernment, and common sense. Where mercy is lacking in attitude or action, we must question if we are truly standing for God or for standards that allow us to be superior to others.

In Job we're discovering that wisdom cannot be reduced to laws. The law is important because it teaches what God's standard is, but it cannot save us. Only a relationship with God can do that. Centuries later Paul, talking about the law, says, "For the letter kills, but the Spirit gives life" (2 Cor. 3:6).

COMPANION THOUGHT

At what age did you think you knew more than your parents and teachers? Has your opinion changed over time? Why?

Job 16

SEARCHING THE HEART

My face is red with weeping, dark shadows ring my eyes, yet my hands have been free of violence, and my prayer is pure.
     Job 16:16–17

JOB WEARIES OF THE ARGUMENTS. He's heard them all before. As he launches into another lengthy lament, we realize he, too, is repeating himself. We begin to wonder, what's the point? Job accuses God of wearing him out (Job 16:7). As readers, we are also being worn out. We recall that Job is a poetic book, a book to be experienced more than analyzed. Job's pain either speaks deeply to us or makes us want to run away.

How we respond has everything to do with where we are in our lives. If things are going well, we may feel impatient with Job's complaints. But if we're suffering, we'll cling to every image, every word. We know what it's like for life to grab us by the neck and crush us against the wall. To burn with shame and anger as others taunt with jeers and judgment. And we identify with Job's need to talk about how we feel. Not just once. But over and over until we have no more words to speak.

When in pain, we may need to talk about our suffering more than others want to hear. Perhaps loved ones say it's time to move on. But when we can't seem to get past our sorrow, Job gives us a safe place to grieve for as long as we need. He gives us the language to express our pain. He also leads us into a deep reflection of the soul that examines our conduct and motives.

A clear conscience strengthens us against the attack of others and gives us confidence to approach God. When we have confessed our sins, we can humbly ask for His strength and wisdom. "Let us then approach God's throne of grace with confidence, so that we may receive mercy and find grace to help us in our time of need" (Heb. 4:16).

COMPANION THOUGHT

How do you grieve? How do you feel when someone tells you it's time to move on? Why? How do you feel when those close to you handle grief differently?

Job 17

SEEKING FOR HOPE

Where then is my hope? Who can see any hope for me?
    Job 17:15

JOB BELIEVES HE HAS NOTHING to look forward to except the grave, darkness, and bodily decay (Job 17:13–14). Still, something within him clings to hope. "My days have passed, my plans are shattered. Yet the desires of my heart turn night into day; in the face of the darkness light is near" (vv. 11–12). Job hopes for some light, even in death.

The capacity to hope in the face of adversity speaks to our resilience as human beings. This instinct is rooted in the character of God. Job's images of light and dark and night and day take us back to creation, where God speaks the world into being. Order and beauty arise from chaos (Gen. 1). The rising and setting of the sun each day, the turning of the seasons, and the cycles of life all witness that there is an end to darkness. There is an end to suffering. Things will change.

In every sunrise, God sends a stunning reminder of new possibilities. In a season of suffering very much like Job's, the author of Lamentations says, "I remember my affliction and my wandering, the bitterness and the gall. I well remember them, and my soul is downcast within me. Yet this I call to mind and therefore I have hope: Because of the LORD's great love we are not consumed, for his compassions never fail. They are new every morning; great is your faithfulness" (Lam. 3:19–23).

Each day we wake up testifies to God's desire to renew. We can either close our eyes to the dawn or welcome the opportunity to see what God will do, to be grateful for what He has already done, and to embrace life, whatever it may bring.

COMPANION THOUGHT

What was your darkest day? How did you feel at that time? And today?

Job 18

A FORGOTTEN MAN

The memory of him perishes from the earth; he has no name in the land.
    Job 18:17

BILDAD STARTS HIS MONOLOGUE BY telling Job to be quiet until he's come to his senses (Job 18:2). What he means is Job should shut up until he comes around to his point of view. Bildad's pride and arrogance tell us his perspective of Job cannot be trusted. The diatribe against a "wicked man" is a thinly veiled way of attacking Job personally. He accuses Job of not knowing God and envisions a terrible end for this suffering man he once called a friend. He predicts that after Job dies, his memory will perish from the earth (Job 18:17).

How ironic that some four thousand years later, we are still studying Job's life, seeking insights into suffering and drawing strength from his example of perseverance. The memory of Job has not perished from the earth. But who is Bildad? Even people familiar with the Bible seldom recognize his name.

Bildad's speech attempts to describe the life of one who does not know God. Instead it reveals our human bent toward self-righteousness. We may find ourselves in Bildad's shoes, very sure we know what is going on in someone else's life. Certain we have the answers. Certain we are wise. But God's wisdom says, "Carry each other's burdens, and in this way you will fulfill the law of Christ. If anyone thinks they are something when they are not, they deceive themselves" (Gal. 6:2–3).

COMPANION THOUGHT

When have you believed something bad about someone and then found out you were mistaken? Why did you believe the worst? How did you find out the truth?

Job 19

A REDEEMER

I know that my redeemer lives.
       Job 19:25

IN ANCIENT TIMES A PERSON destroyed by famine, war, or sickness had no safety net. The only hope for the destitute was a redeemer. A redeemer, usually a wealthy close relative, could buy back the family's assets from creditors and restore the family's reputation.[19] The redeemer would also defend the family from legal action by redressing any wrongs. Job concludes that no human relative will come to his defense (Job 19:3–17), but his despair turns his gaze upward. He insists that a divine redeemer will intervene on his behalf. Unknowingly, he announces the redeemer of all mankind, Jesus (v. 25).

Nowhere in Scripture do we see a more courageous stance of faith. Stripped of all he has, forsaken and condemned by his family and friends, and feeling abandoned by God, Job proclaims that somehow, someway, the divine redeemer will come to his rescue. Though death hovers near, Job refuses to believe that death ends life. He says, "And after my skin has been destroyed, yet in my flesh I will see God; I myself will see him with my own eyes" (vv. 26–27).

Job is on an emotional roller coaster, but he keeps coming back to his faith. Confidence in his friends and the religion they once held in common has proven unreliable. But now he reaches for God. Looking to Him as his redeemer, he finds hope.

Job warns us to be careful how we judge, because one day the sword of judgment will fall on us all. We will answer for our words and for our lives. On that day we will grieve over the hurts we've caused (Matt 12:36; Heb. 9:27).[20] Though God will make us aware of these sins, He will pardon those of us who have accepted Jesus through faith (Acts 4:12). For believers a coming judgment reminds us of the great debt Christ has paid. Our sins past, present, and future are covered by His blood. Such forgiveness compels us to extend the grace God is giving us to others. Our job is not to condemn but to point hurting people to the hope Christ offers.

COMPANION THOUGHT

Who do you call when you have financial problems? Does their attitude make you feel better or worse? How do you think God views you when you need help? Why?

*I know that my redeemer lives,
and that in the end
he will stand on the earth.*

JOB 19:25

Job 20

ZOPHAR'S ANGRY RESPONSE

I hear a rebuke that dishonors me.
 Job 20:3

JOB TOLD HIS FRIENDS, "YOU should fear the sword yourselves" (Job 19:29). His rebuke arouses Zophar's fury. Insulted by the suggestion that God would judge them, Zophar turns the subject of God's wrath back onto Job. He lumps Job in with those full of pride, who oppress the poor and seize the homes and property of others. Zophar is mistaken about Job, but his warning to the wicked has merit.

A person who defies God and oppresses the weak has every reason to tremble. In the Bible multiple stories are being told at the same time—personal stories (such as Job and his accusers), God's story (revealing a plan to redeem our world), and our story. The Holy Spirit highlights the truths we need to hear. Zophar's accusations, while inappropriate for Job, may convict us if we are grappling with unconfessed sin.

Hebrews 4:12 says, "For the word of God is alive and active. Sharper than any double-edged sword, it penetrates even to dividing soul and spirit, joints and marrow; it judges the thoughts and attitudes of the heart." As we read God's Word, the Holy Spirit makes us aware of what applies to our specific situation. God's wisdom is found in the right words, spoken at the right time, to the right person. The messenger may be arrogant and judgmental, but if the message is one we need to hear, we would be wise to pay attention.

COMPANION THOUGHT

What kind of comment immediately starts an argument in your house? Do you usually defuse or inflame it? How?

Job 21

WHY DO THE WICKED PROSPER?

Why do the wicked live on, growing old and increasing in power?
    Job 21:7

JOB ASKS QUESTIONS WE ALL want answers to: Why do the godly suffer? Why do the wicked prosper? At this point, both Job and his friends believe that retribution theology should govern the world. They agree good should prosper and the wicked should suffer. But they differ in their conclusions. The sages insist that because God is just, His world must operate according to the laws of justice. Job takes the opposite position—those who suffer don't always deserve it. We're with him so far. It's the conclusion he's working toward that chills us—the innocent suffer; therefore, God must be unjust. If this is true, the foundation of faith crumbles.

This fear tends to keep us (like Job's friends) firmly entrenched in our belief systems. We hide behind religious and moral traditions, narrowing our vision to situations that support our view. Job calls us out. "Have you never questioned those who travel?" (Job 21:29), he asks. In other words, you need a bigger worldview. A belief system that denies that the innocent suffer is naive. It's foolish. It's false.

Deep down we know faith must be built on truth. The reality of a suffering world cannot be ignored. Questioning is better than blindly believing something that isn't true. Our vulnerability makes us desperate for and open to the revelation of God.

John 16:13 says that the Holy Spirit will lead us into all truth. We rely on this as we journey with Job into our own suffering.

COMPANION THOUGHT

How do you respond to people of faith who seem to have an answer for everything? What value is there in seeking answers if some things can't be known?

Job 22

GOOD ADVICE THAT DOES LITTLE GOOD

Submit to God and be at peace with him.
   Job 22:21

JOB'S FRIENDS NO LONGER SEE him as a good man who has sinned, as one who only needs to repent and be restored—they view him as an utterly wicked person. Eliphaz, dropping all pretense of civility, accuses Job of demanding security of his relatives, stripping the poor, withholding food and water from the needy, and taking advantage of widows and orphans (Job 22:6–9). Job's friends sacrifice Job on the altar of their neatly packaged theology. Not once do they consider that their beliefs could be wrong.

Eliphaz, completely mistaken in his assessment of Job, again offers advice that under other circumstances could've been encouraging: "Submit to God and be at peace with him." Perhaps Job could've received these words had they been offered in love. But the condemnation of his friends has erected a barrier. Once he would've looked to them for counsel, but he will soon shut them out.

The wisdom of God has always been more than words. Timing, context, and motive all matter. God's wisdom encompasses more than theology, more than the law, even more than justice. As we wonder how this can be, we edge closer to the heart of the book of Job and the heart of God.

When we are tempted to judge and are sure we have the answers to someone else's problems, it is time to look deeper. Or perhaps inward. Proverbs reminds us that "a gentle answer turns away wrath, but a harsh word stirs up anger" (Prov. 15:1). We are called to uphold God's standards with compassion, gentleness, and humility. "Do nothing out of selfish ambition or vain conceit. Rather, in humility value others above yourselves" (Phil. 2:3–4).

COMPANION THOUGHT

When you were a child, did your father or mother yell back when verbally attacked? Shut down? Leave? Get even? Cry? Try to reason or appease? Back down? Not respond? How did you react then? How do you react now when attacked?

Job 23

THE GOODNESS OF GOD

But he knows the way that I take; when he has tested me, I will come forth as gold.
    Job 23:10

JOB, TORTURED IN BODY AND mind, reaches for God, but God seems far away. Job laments, "If only I know where to find him. . . . I would state my case before him" (Job 23:3–4). Emotionally, Job has been up and down. His rants have bordered on hysteria. But now we feel a slight shift as Job averts his attention from his friends and toward God. He will continue to engage but no longer seems desperate to win them over.

The faith that he claimed from the start settles him. A new perspective of his suffering takes shape as Job realizes he is not experiencing God's abandonment but God's testing. We know this because we were privy to the discussion between God and the Accuser in the heavenly court (Job 1). Now Job sees it too. He feels no sense of God's presence but believes God is working in his life (vv. 8–10). Though the issue of justice has not been addressed, Job digs deeper to a grounding faith.

A demand for fairness can rob us of peace and hope. God invites our questions, but what we most need may not be answers but a shaking up of beliefs that keep us from knowing Him. Suffering reveals the inadequacy of man-made theologies.

Our culture claims all we need is within us. False religions say God will give us whatever we ask for, whatever we can envision. But pain proves them liars. When life fails, we are more likely to question these paradigms. Then desperation serves a purpose—it directs us away from our human systems to the person of Jesus Christ. Even if we do not feel the Lord is near, God asks us to trust in His goodness. Job is our example. Despite his suffering, he believes God will see him through. "But [God] knows the way that I take; when he has tested me, I will come forth as gold" (v. 10). This is Job's hope and ours.

COMPANION THOUGHT

What is one thing you used to believe about God that you no longer believe? What changed your mind?

But he knows the way that I take;
when he has tested me,
I will come forth as gold.

JOB 23:10

Job 24

WHY DOES GOD ALLOW EVIL?

Why does the Almighty not set times for judgment?
    Job 24:1

JOB CANNOT UNDERSTAND HOW a just God can see evil winning and do nothing about it. The lack of justice in the world plunges Job into depression. He can't let go of it. Nor can we. Why? What is it that makes us evaluate every situation as fair or unfair? That stirs us to rebellion and war when we see injustice? That compels us to call out people, family members, and institutions we see taking advantage? That looks for, even expects, someone to object to the wrongs in our world?

The need for justice is woven into our DNA. That baseline—a longing for equity—reflects the character of our Maker. Scripture teaches God is just (Isa. 61:8) and we are made in His image (Gen 1:26). Injustice makes us scream *this should not be!* Yet we ourselves fall short of God's standard. We apply justice inconsistently, pursuing it when the scales tip in our favor, ignoring it when it does not. Still, the conviction that the wicked should be punished and the innocent should be vindicated runs in our veins.

How do we square this with reality? We question. We struggle with God. In this context, the act of questioning may be seen as holy work. Though we may vacillate between faith and disillusionment, the refusal to accept pat answers pushes us deeper. Incapacitated, Job can do little but sit. And think. And observe. And wrestle. This kind of contemplation is exactly what is needed when we are sorting out the foundations of faith. The Bible says, "Continue to work out your salvation with fear and trembling" (Phil. 2:12).

COMPANION THOUGHT

If you knew there was no judgment day or afterlife, would you live your life differently? Why or why not?

Job 25

A RHETORICAL QUESTION?

How then can a mortal be righteous before God?
    Job 25:4

HOW CAN WE BE RIGHTEOUS before God? Bildad asks his question rhetorically, thinking he knows the answer—it's impossible. His wisdom says that mortals can never be righteous before God. But his claims are based on two assumptions—first, that human beings are like maggots in God's sight, and second, that it is up to us to forge the path to God and earn His favor. He's wrong on both counts.

The Bible does say that our own righteousness is as filthy rags (Isa. 64:6). However, it also teaches we have intrinsic value. We are made in God's image. Having placed humans high in the order of created beings, our Creator has crowned us with glory and honor (Ps. 8:3–6).

It has never been our job to bridge the gap between God and mortals. This has been the LORD's territory from the beginning. God initiated fellowship with Adam and Eve (Gen. 1:26–28). In time He will make Abraham's family great as a way of revealing Himself to the world (Gen. 12:1–3). He will rescue the Israelites from bondage, institute a sacrificial system for the forgiveness of sins, and establish Israel as a nation (Ex. 14:30; Ex. 24–31; 2 Sam. 7:24). Bildad, unaware of the ongoing redemptive work of God, sees no way we can be reconciled to Him. God knows what Bildad does not—a plan is in place. His Son will be the pathway by which anyone may come to God. Jesus is the divine answer to Bildad's question.

In difficult circumstances, pride presses for an explanation, but humility accepts that our wisdom is incomplete. We do not know how God is working out His purposes in our lives and world today, but the Bible says, "No eye has seen, no ear has heard, and no mind has imagined what God has prepared for those who love him" (1 Cor. 2:9 NLT).

COMPANION THOUGHT

Do you tend to think of yourself as a "worm" or "beloved?" Why?

Job 26

AN ANGRY RESPONSE

How you have helped the powerless!
    Job 26:2

JOB HAS PUSHED BACK ALL along, but a rush of poetic sarcasm gives us the cathartic moment we've longed for. He says (paraphrasing), "How helpful Bildad is! What wonderful advice he gives! What compassion, intelligence, and wisdom he displays for the ignorant!" We don't blame Job for attacking his friends as they've attacked him. The author makes no judgment about it. We recognize a common response to suffering—lashing out. We, too, are prone to doing this, especially when others don't understand. Again, Job gives us language to express our frustration. He asks Bildad, "Who has helped you utter these words?" Job's final shot implies that Bildad's words come from the pit of hell. Certainly not from God.

Job ends his poem with a vivid description of the Creator's power. The contrast between the shallow wisdom of his friends and the great wisdom of God becomes obvious. We see that Job is not fighting against God, whose power and mystery cannot be matched. He's fighting against his friends, who claim to understand how God's power relates to his suffering. He says, "The realm of the dead is naked before God; destruction lies uncovered" (Job 26:6). The implication? No one can hide from God. The LORD sees the harm they are doing to him.

Understanding that God continuously watches over the world He created humbles Job and should humble us. We see only the edges, "the outer fringes" of God's work (v. 14), yet creation whispers, *God is LORD of all. Listen closely. He is near.*

COMPANION THOUGHT

How should knowing God is all powerful and that He sees how others treat you affect your response to injustice?

Job 27

A DYING MAN'S RESOLUTION

As long as I live, while I have breath from God, my lips will speak no evil, and my tongue will speak no lies.
    Job 27:3–4 NLT

AS JOB FACES WHAT APPEARS to be the end of his life, he commits to truth. He won't say things that will harm or deceive another, he won't lie, and he won't deny what he knows to be true. He says, "I will maintain my innocence and never let go of it" (Job 27:6). Job isn't saying he's blameless because he's never sinned but that whatever sins he's committed have been atoned for. His claim of innocence rests on the work of God.

Job's piety has not been hypocritical—he's lived his life doing what honors God. How? Primarily by treating others justly. The irony that God, who stands for justice, denies it to him is not lost on him. We hear the barb in his complaint (v. 2). Job cannot reconcile a just God with his situation, but neither can he accept that God is unjust.

To hold to our integrity while grappling with God requires a continual returning to what we know to be true about Him. From creation through Israel's story, God has revealed himself to be loving, kind, good, patient, merciful, and yes—just. Though our reality may not square with this, we can hold to what the Bible says. The New Testament affirms Job's conviction that a terrible fate awaits the wicked and the righteous will be rewarded (John 3:16). But when? Time is running out for Job. What is the basis of Job's confidence that justice will yet prevail? A faint hope stirs . . . Perhaps hope extends beyond this life?

We long for justice in this life, but if our all-wise God does not grant it, justice will be meted out in the world to come.[21] However, this future reckoning doesn't mean there is no help for today. The psalmist says, "I remain confident of this: I will see the goodness of the LORD in the land of the living. Wait for the LORD; be strong and take heart and wait for the LORD. His comfort and sustaining power is available to us in the land of the living" (Ps. 27:13–14).

COMPANION THOUGHT

What about life after death most appeals to you? No more tears? The rewards? Seeing justice served? Being with loved ones? Why?

Job 28

THE SEARCH FOR WISDOM

Where then does wisdom come from? Where does understanding dwell?
   Job 28:20

THIS INTERLUDE STRIKES A DIFFERENT tone from Job's arguments so far. The emotional language is gone. So is the sparring. This passage is calm, objective rather than personal. It is not clear if Job continues to speak or if the author interrupts Job's discourse, but the change in tone and style catches our attention. Job is no longer the center of attention. Abruptly the interlude pulls us away from suffering and toward the book's main theme—wisdom.

The description of a man mining for riches challenges us to pursue wisdom with the same fervor we pursue wealth. The narrator observes:

- We human beings are remarkably creative and persevering when it comes to acquiring wealth.(Job 28:3–4)
- Ingenuity and hard work are required to gain anything of value. (v. 9–11)
- Wisdom is of more value than any earthly treasure. (v. 13–19)
- No matter how hard we apply our resources, abilities, ingenuity, perseverance, and strength, we can never attain wisdom apart from God. (v. 28)

The sage concludes that wisdom is not in the deep, not in the sea, not in the wisdom of the sages. Wisdom is found in God alone.[22] Though the LORD may grant wisdom to nonbelievers (just as He gives air, light, and rain to all creation), He is wisdom's source.[23] However, godly wisdom remains godly only if rooted in the fear of the LORD (Prov. 9:10). Nonbelievers may have wise instincts, but without a commitment to a biblical standard, they may make different choices than believers. They view life from an earthy perspective, the believer from the eternal.

What does this mean for Job and those of us who suffer? We ask the LORD to help us view our pain through the lens of His wisdom.

COMPANION THOUGHT

Would you ask a wise person who was not a believer if you should tithe or marry an unbeliever? Why or why not?

*The fear of the L<small>ORD</small>—that is wisdom,
and to shun evil is understanding.*

JOB 28:28

Job 29

JOB REMEMBERS BETTER DAYS

Oh, for the days when I was in my prime.
    Job 29:4

THE LIFE JOB HAD KNOWN before calamity struck shimmers before him like a dream. He sees himself surrounded by family, respected by the community, and loved by those he'd helped over the years. Everything he touched prospered back then. People listened to him. Job says, "How I long for the months gone by, for the days when God watched over me" (Job 29:2). But now, he feels God no longer sees or cares. It's not just the reversal of fortune, but the Lord's absence that guts him.

We understand. We, too, struggle with disappointment with God. The book begins to address this disillusionment here, but not in the way we'd expect. Chapters 29–31 take us on a retrospective of Job's life. With remembering comes perspective. For twenty-nine chapters we've been on the ash heap with Job, feeling his terror, anger, and frustration through the lens of our own suffering. But we also have the vantage point of the heavenly court. Much is going on behind the scenes Job is unaware of. We know that Job is innocent. This assurance, both vindicating and unsettling, pushes toward an even higher perspective—that of the New Testament. Christ will teach that suffering can be a redemptive act. A transforming act. But for now, we must walk with Job as if we did not know. Our task is to gather the lessons learned in the dark:

- *Life is complex.* Any theology that views the world simplistically is foolish.
- *Our vision is limited.* If we think we see all there is to see, we are ignorant.
- *God is present.* Pain and exhaustion may cause us to lose the sense of God's presence, but He is with us.

COMPANION THOUGHT

How much time do you spend thinking about the past? Do you think it was better or worse than your present? Why?

Job 30

A HUMBLING REVERSAL

But now they mock me.
    Job 30:1

JOB TURNS FROM THE PAST to the present. His life, once marked by blessing and prosperity, now reeks of humiliation. Not only are health, family, friends, possessions, resources, and influence gone, but people are taking advantage of his situation. Those who once vied for his favor now mock him. This loss of respect seems to bother him most. We hear a tone of superiority in Job's opinion of the young men who now ridicule him. He describes them as worthless youths whose fathers he wouldn't have allowed to sleep with the dogs (Job 30:1). His attitude reflects the ugly side of retribution theology—entitlement.

Job believes he deserves better. He feels his relationship with God and his good works entitle him to blessing and prosperity. It may not be how God runs the world, but it should be. Entitlement forces this question: Do we want God to give us what we deserve?

The Scriptures have made clear that "there is no one who does good, not even one" (Ps. 14:3). Romans 6:23 says, "For the wages of sin is death." This puts us in a precarious place. If we insist on justice, we condemn ourselves. Apart from God, we are all like the worthless youths Job despises. Despise them, and we despise ourselves.

Without mercy no one can stand before God. Jeremiah reminds us that "because of the LORD's great love, we are not consumed, for his compassions never fail" (Lam. 3:22). Whatever hope we have is not in God's judgment but in His mercy.

COMPANION THOUGHT

What three things do you think you deserve? Why? Do you offer them to those you love? To strangers? Why or why not?

Job 31

INNOCENCE

Oh, that I had someone to hear me! I sign now my defense—let the Almighty answer me.
    Job 31:35

JOB REVIEWS HOW HE'S LIVED his life. He insists he is not guilty of the things his friends have accused him of. To prove it, he checks off behaviors we recognize that meet the standards of morality found in the law, Proverbs, and the teachings of Jesus.[24] He hasn't lusted after other women. Hasn't lied. He's treated others with respect, helped the poor, and defended widows and orphans. He hasn't served false gods. He hasn't trusted in his wealth or coveted what others have, but he has opened his home and shared his bounty with others.

Job presents himself as righteous based on his works. But didn't we just read that no one is righteous? Hasn't Job questioned God to the point of blasphemy? And what of his attitudes of entitlement and superiority? Those sound like sin to us. Does God view Job as righteous despite those things? The answer is yes. Not because of Job's works, but his faith.

God has always imparted grace to those who put their trust in Him. In Job's time the understanding that believers take on the Christ's righteousness is centuries away. The faithful, then, are justified in advance of Jesus's sacrifice—"on credit," we could say. Job's sins past, present, and future are covered by Jesus's blood, even if he lacks understanding of that. Job correctly says, "Let God weigh me in honest scales and he will know that I am blameless" (Job 31:6). God agrees.

However, the Bible also teaches that being pure before God is a continuing process. Jesus says, "Be perfect, therefore, as your heavenly Father is perfect" (Matt. 5:48). A better translation for perfect is "complete." God does not expect we will never sin—He expects us to stay in relationship with Him, where the Holy Spirit, revealing our sin, can forgive, purify, and make us whole again.

COMPANION THOUGHT

What two things do you *not* do that alerts others that you are a follower of Jesus?

Job 32

ELIHU SPEAKS

It is the spirit in a person, the breath of the Almighty, that gives them understanding.
   Job 32:8

AS THE DEBATE COMES TO a close, Elihu steps forward. He has a Hebrew name and heritage. In the story, his relative Buz is Abraham's nephew (Gen. 22:20–22). Elihu means *my God is He* or *He remains God*. If the previous speakers represent the best of ancient Near Eastern thought, then Elihu represents Jewish orthodoxy. Both perspectives would've been important in an Israelite debate on wisdom, where Job's story might have been told centuries later.[25] Compared to ancient traditions, Mosaic law (like Elihu) is a newcomer. But Elihu's reference to the "breath of the Almighty" takes us back to creation. God, the source of wisdom, existed before the law.[26]

Remember the eloquent discourse on wisdom we read in chapter 28, with its mining metaphor? Job's review of his life followed it, bringing his plight to the forefront again. Now the author connects the two. As readers we're being invited to mine Elihu's words for wisdom. Elihu's five-chapter speech gives us plenty of raw material. We've not found wisdom in the tradition of man. Will we find it in the tradition of Moses?

Elihu is younger than Job's friends. According to custom, this would make his words less weighty. However, Elihu says, "It is not only the old who are wise, not only the aged who understand what is right" (Job 32:9). Perhaps what he says is true, but he insults both Job and his friends. Elihu's blustery introduction, full of self-importance, raises a red flag. Can we trust him? The Bible says to "test everything that is said" (1 Thess. 5:21 NLT). Words that lack hope are not from God. God says, "For I know the plans I have for you . . . plans to prosper you and not to harm you, plans to give you hope and a future" (Jer. 29:11).

COMPANION THOUGHT

How does the law of Moses impact how you live your life?

Job 33

WHO DO WE LISTEN TO?

Pay attention, Job, and listen to me.
    Job 33:31

ELIHU RIGHTLY DESCRIBES HIMSELF AS "full of words" (Job 32:18). It takes him twenty-four verses to tell us he's going to speak. But we can't dismiss him. He brings some perspectives we need to hear. Elihu says he has a right to speak because he is human. As a person gifted with the breath of Almighty God, he deserves a voice. Elihu is saying, "I am not better than you. I, too, have been taken from the clay [v. 6]; but neither am I inferior to you." However, his arrogance immediately undermines his case. This pattern will prove characteristic.

Elihu claims he's listened carefully to Job's words, but his conclusion proves he has not. Job has never said he is without sin. Rather, Job feared God held former sins against him (Job 7:21). Job did claim to be godly and to have lived in right relationship with God. His statements of innocence should've been taken in that context.

Elihu judges Job wrongly. However, he observes two things that are true—God speaks to people in many ways, and He may allow adversity to save us from greater harm. The problem is, neither of these applies to Job. Elihu concludes this passage with one of the most arrogant statements in Scripture: "Be silent, and I will teach you wisdom" (Job 33:33). Elihu isn't even privy to the heavenly court, let alone the perspective of God.

Pride will keep us from listening well. If we lack humility, we are prone to mistaken assumptions. If we recognize pride in another, we must put their words into perspective. Truth alone is not wisdom. Wisdom calls for truth to be applied in the right way, at the right time, to the right person.

COMPANION THOUGHT

Who do you know who is "full of words"? How do you feel about spending time with them? Do you listen to them? Why or why not?

The Spirit of God has made me; the breath of the Almighty gives me life.

JOB 33:4

Job 34

TEST THE WORDS YOU HEAR

The ear tests words as the tongue tastes food.
    Job 34:3

ELIHU ASKS US TO CONSIDER carefully what he is saying. We've heard conflicting arguments. Obviously, they can't all be correct. The ear must hear them all, then discern. Just as we judge what is good or harmful to our bodies by tasting the foods that go into our mouths, we must evaluate what others claim is true before accepting it. We will need to filter Elihu's many words.

He begins with the mistaken assumption that Job is guilty, followed by a misstatement of fact. Job never said, "There is no profit in trying to please God" (Job 34:9); He was quoting the wicked (Job 21:15). Elihu mischaracterizes Job's words while ignoring his statements of faith. Ironically, amid these distortions, Elihu gives an inspired overview of the tenets of orthodox belief: God can do no wrong (Job 34:10); God is just (vv. 11–12); God is the giver and sustainer of life (v. 15); God controls everything (vv. 18–30); God determines how we come to him (vv. 31–33).

Elihu reminds us that truth seldom comes to us in a pure form. A person can be wise in some ways and foolish in others. As humans we are a mass of contradictions, and so are the churches, institutions, and social structures we create. Truth must be sorted out. We test the words we hear by asking:

- *Are they truthful and accurate?* Can the "facts" be documented?
- *What effect do they have on others?* Are they kind, fair, appropriate?
- *Do they follow godly principles?* Single verses can be easily taken out of context, but God affirms His truth many times throughout the entire Bible.

COMPANION THOUGHT

If someone puts food in front of you that you've not had before, what factors affect whether you will try it (taste, smell, who prepared it, the occasion, etc.)? In matters of faith, what determines whether you will believe something?

Job 35

DOES GOD CARE?

How much less, then, will he listen when you say that you do not see him.
    Job 35:14

IN THE PREVIOUS CHAPTER, ELIHU repeated the mantra of Job's friends: "[God] repays everyone for what they have done; he brings on them what their conduct deserves" (Job 34:11). Because Job challenges this simplistic view of God's sovereignty, Elihu has turned on him. He wished more suffering on Job to cure him of his rebellion (Job 34:36–37).

Now, the young man presumes to know what God thinks and how He works. Again, we find some truth—what we do neither adds to nor detracts from God's wholeness—but Elihu's portrayal of God as indifferent and uncaring is inaccurate.

The people of Job's day had no Scriptures to vet their beliefs. But the Jewish sages studying Job's story years later do. In making rigid laws out of general principles found in Proverbs, they've effectively turned the Word of God into the tradition of men. This distortion breeds arrogance and error. Elihu's belief that he has sufficient knowledge and perspective to judge leads him to misrepresent both Job and God.

Elihu claims God doesn't hear the cries of the oppressed because they are wicked.[27] He puts Job in this category. He takes Job's anguished admission that he cannot see God as proof (Job 35:12–14). Should we trust Elihu? Fortunately, we don't have to depend on a person's opinion of God to learn what He is like. The LORD has given us the Bible. The stories of people who have engaged with Him reveal many facets of His character.

The author of Job shows us a God who gives us great latitude to express our emotions. Who allows us to question. Who does not judge us while we're in the process of getting to know Him and His ways. Scripture tells us that the Lord "heals the brokenhearted and binds up their wounds" (Ps. 147:3). The Bible assures us that while we may not see God, He sees us and cares. Who will we believe?

COMPANION THOUGHT

When do you tend to repeat yourself and talk more than you should? When you're angry? Frustrated? Nervous? Happy? Do you realize it at the time? How do you think overtalking affects how others see you? How God sees you?

Job 36

ELIHU'S CLAIMS

There is more to be said in God's behalf.
     Job 36:2

WHERE JOB'S OTHER FRIENDS SPOKE with authority based on ancient wisdom, common knowledge, and tradition, Elihu claims to speak on behalf of God. His eloquent discourse on God's goodness, justice, and power tempts us to believe him. But knowing that God has declared Job righteous forces us to look beyond the young man's words to the way he uses them.

Elihu's monologue about God comes after another "objective" reflection on the righteous versus the wicked. It's meant to condemn Job. Elihu drives this home in verses 16 and 17: "He is wooing you from the jaws of distress to a spacious place free from restriction. . . . But now you are laden with the judgment due the wicked; judgment and justice have taken hold of you." In other words, "You're wicked, but God is trying to give you a second chance." From this arrogant perspective, Elihu lectures us on God's greatness.

By demonstrating a grasp of God's character and works, Elihu seeks credibility. His words in another context could and have been used as worship. But here they are self-serving, meant to add weight to Elihu's opinion, not to praise God.

The dynamic between Job, Elihu, and God demonstrates that wisdom must consider timing, context, and attitude. "But the wisdom that comes from heaven is first of all pure; then peace-loving, considerate, submissive, full of mercy and good fruit, impartial and sincere" (James 3:17).

COMPANION THOUGHT

Describe a time when someone claimed to know what God wanted you to do. How did you react? Why? When you feel God gives you a word for someone else, do you think you should tell them? Why? If so, how?

Job 37

IS GOD BEYOND US?

The Almighty is beyond our reach and exalted in power.
   Job 37:23

ELIHU IS A POWERFUL ORATOR. The "listen" in verse 2, a plural Hebrew verb, indicates he's addressing a gathering of people. He holds our attention with his emotional description of God's control of the forces of nature.

As brash as he is, Elihu has a prophetic gift. There is truth in what he says. God's wisdom, power, and justice do exceed our human limitations. "The Almighty is beyond our reach and exalted in power; in his justice and great righteousness, he does not oppress" (Job 37:23). We may not understand why God is dealing with us as He is but we can be confident He is righteous and just.

Elihu's perspective is a good one, so why does it bring little comfort? Perhaps because it is incomplete. It fails to consider God's love for us. Though His ways and knowledge are beyond our reach, He Himself is not. This mysterious and fantastic truth defies our human comprehension. God's love isn't limited by our mental capacity.

When we're on the ground wounded and helpless, words alone seldom reach us. We long for touch. We want to know that someone sees and cares. Elihu chastises Job for wanting to speak to God. It's not God's word Job is after, but God's presence. But does God chastise us for coming to Him? We're about to find out. Elihu's arguments bring the debates to a close and set the stage for the appearance of God, who speaks directly to Job for the first time.

COMPANION THOUGHT

When you are in great pain, do you most long for someone to talk to you? Hold you? Cry with you? Help in practical ways? Or do you prefer to be left alone? Why?

Job 38

GOD SPEAKS

*Then the L*ORD *answered Job.*
     Job 38:1 NLT

THROUGHOUT HIS ORDEAL, JOB DESIRED a hearing with God. He cried, "Oh, that I had someone to hear me! . . . let the Almighty answer me!" (Job 31:35). At last God grants his request. The debates are over. The crowd is gone. To our surprise, God says nothing about suffering or justice. Rather, He offers a series of rhetorical questions that challenge the underlying assumption made by Job and his friends—that they have a big enough perspective to comment on how He runs the world.

Taking Job on a virtual tour of the universe, the architect of heaven and earth opens Job's eyes to the complexities of the world. God's attention to every detail showcases His wisdom. His point? Suffering cannot be viewed only from the perspective of our limited life experience.

Still, the LORD speaks to Job "out of the storm" (Job 38:1).[28] It is often as the chaos of life swirls around us that we hear God's voice. Later, the LORD will give Job the opportunity to answer, but for now God overwhelms him with questions. They are not intended to make Job feel insignificant but to reveal we can't begin to understand what goes into running and sustaining the world.

A proper understanding of who God is and who we are is absolutely necessary for any meaningful engagement of faith. The Mosaic law and stories of God's intervention in Israel's past have shown us that God is powerful, holy, wise, good, just, and merciful. We are God's beloved but not His equal. We are sin filled and helpless. If we are in a season that leaves us speechless, we can be sure God is speaking—and we are to listen.

COMPANION THOUGHT

What famous person would you like to meet with for an hour? Why this person? What would you want to discuss? What would you want to ask God?

*Where were you when I
laid the earth's foundation?*

JOB 38:4

Job 39

OUR LIMITED PERSPECTIVE

Does the eagle soar at your command and build his nest on high?
   Job 39:27

THIS CHAPTER TURNS OUR GAZE from the heavenlies toward the earth. God's involvement in sustaining all forms of life on our earth is as stunning as His creation of the sun, moon, and stars. We feel His delight in and concern for all living things. We cannot help but contrast His awesome display of wisdom and power to Job's finite capacities. If human beings cannot control nature or sustain all that lives on earth, how can we understand the mysteries of life?

While God does not directly address suffering, He gives us a framework for dealing with it. The LORD's approach is very different from that of Job's friends. Elihu condemns Job with poetic pronouncements. God asks questions that allow Job to search his heart. Elihu's words were meant to crush. God's words restore.

However, there is a missing piece of the "suffering" puzzle that explains why a full discussion of pain is not found here or elsewhere in the Old Testament—Christ has not yet come. His death on the cross will show us that suffering can redeem. We glimpse it when Joseph tells his brothers, "You intended to harm me, but God intended it for good" (Gen. 50:20). Elihu hints at it when he lists reasons why God allows pain (Job 33:14–30). But the knowledge of both men is incomplete.

Not until Jesus comes do we see suffering transformed into glory. New Testament writers make the connection in books like 2 Corinthians and 1 Peter. For now, God shows us that when we don't understand, we have every reason to trust. The Creator of the universe daily sustains His world, and He can sustain us.

COMPANION THOUGHT

Imagine trying to explain to a child why you cannot put a broken egg back together. What limitations do you and the child have that would make this difficult? How does this illustration reflect our inability to understand suffering?

Job 40

SILENCED BEFORE GOD

Will the one who contends with the Almighty correct him? Let him who accuses God answer him.
　　Job 40:2

JOB'S QUESTIONS EVAPORATE AS AWARENESS of who God is engulfs him. A nod to God as Creator is one thing. An encounter with God is another. Job stammers, "I am unworthy" (Job 40:4). But God has more to say. Remember what started the debate? The disconnect between Job's suffering and the belief that God always rewards the good and punishes the wicked. In making the general God-given principles of Proverbs laws, the sages have preached a theology of retribution that misrepresents God and condemns those who suffer.

God challenges Job to clothe himself in splendor and put himself in God's place. God is saying, *You run things for a day. Go ahead—bring down every proud and wicked person in the world.* Perhaps we squirm, thinking of our own struggles with pride and sin. At some point we realize that if we insist the world be run according to the strict laws of justice, we condemn ourselves. Is this what we want? In case Job is still inclined to answer yes, God evokes the image of a beast common in ancient Near Eastern mythology—the behemoth. In the next chapter, He'll call forth a second one, the Leviathan. They represent what cannot be controlled by mortal man.

The behemoth is wild, dangerous, "yet its Maker can approach it with his sword" (v. 19). A dumb beast knows not to resist its Creator, even if the Creator's intent is to kill it. We, however, not only resist the Creator God, but we also challenge Him. We correct Him. By now we should be trembling alongside Job. Our questions seem irrelevant. We cannot control our own lives. Do we think we can control God's universe? Perhaps our hearts sink as we realize we cannot.

The Lord alone is all wise. All powerful. But though He runs the world, He will not take Lordship of our hearts by force. If we want Him to be God in our lives, we must relinquish control.

COMPANION THOUGHT

Have you ever insisted you could do something, then couldn't do it? How did you feel about it? Did you ask someone to help you? Why or why not?

Job 41

GOD'S LEVIATHAN

Who then is able to stand against me?
   Job 41:10

THE LEVIATHAN AND BEHEMOTH, WELL-KNOWN creatures from ancient Near Eastern mythology, evoke awe and fear. Western minds feel compelled to tame them. It's been suggested the behemoth is a hippopotamus and the Leviathan a crocodile. Another theory is that they are extinct animals. The behemoth is mentioned only in Job, but the Leviathan appears elsewhere in Scripture (Isa. 27:1; Ps. 74:14; Ps. 104:26). Real or imagined, these beasts symbolize the nature of our world—awesome in its order and beauty yet wild and dangerous. Like these two creatures, our world is not safe, but it is good. This reality humbles us.

Our logic has limits. Our physical bodies have limits. Our sight, our perspectives, our experiences have limits. But God expands our capacity with His presence and the language of poetry. God's face-to-face with Job concludes with the image of these two beasts roaming the world. They aren't seen as evil but as free creatures who enjoy God's bounty, though they are hunted and feared. As we watch the Leviathan cut through the water, leaving a glistening wake, God whispers that we live in an amazing, complex world. For now, it includes suffering. But God is in control. Standing against the dangers of life shouldn't worry us, but standing against God should. He asks, "Who has a claim against me that I must pay? Everything under heaven belongs to me" (Job 41:11).

COMPANION THOUGHT

If you ran the world for one day, what one thing you would do? What possible negative impact would it have? Who would be angry? Who would benefit? Would it be fair to everyone? Why or why not?

Job 42

GRACE WINS

When Job prayed for his friends, the Lord restored his fortunes.
Job 42:10 NLT

JOB RETURNS TO THE ASH heap once again, this time in repentance. He is not guilty of what his friends accused him of, but he has been insubordinate with God. In ignorance he'd questioned God's justice and His character. Now he admits, "I know that you can do all things; no purpose of yours can be thwarted" (Job 42:2). Job is still destitute, without family or friends, and in physical pain, but his encounter with the Lord transforms him. Making no demands, Job humbly submits to the wisdom, authority, and care of God.

The Lord rebukes the three friends for accusing Job of wrongdoing. He ignores Elihu—perhaps giving his youthful brashness a pass,—but orders the elder sages to offer atoning sacrifices. In an ironic twist, God commands Job to pray for his friends. After Job prays, God forgives their offenses and blesses Job in double measure. The phrase "restored his fortune" in verse 10 also translates as "turned" or "removed the captivity" of Job (KJV). We remember that Job, though blessed, had been living under a cloud of fear. Now he is free. God also restores his health and his fortune. These blessings are not payoffs for righteousness, as retribution theology would suggest. They are gifts of grace.

The book of Job reveals that God alone is wise. Insisting on answers tempts us either to rely on insufficient, simplistic principles or to accuse God based on our limited knowledge. He approves of our wrestling with Him, of asking the hard questions. We're allowed to cry out and express our frustration. But in the end, it's His presence that comforts us. There, answers are irrelevant. We don't need to know why we suffer, only that we are safe in God's arms.

COMPANION THOUGHT

What quality of God's have you failed to appreciate? Why? What is the one thing you wish others appreciated about you? Do you think God is more concerned with your good qualities or your faults? Why?

*I know that you can do all things;
no purpose of yours can be thwarted.*

JOB 42:2

RESOURCES

FORTY SIGNIFICANT PEOPLE OF THE BIBLE CHART

Antediluvian Period (Before the Flood)	Patriarchal Period	The Exodus Giving of Law Conquest of Canaan	Period of the Judges	Period of The United Kingdom
Dates Unknown	APPROXIMATE DATES 2200–1800 BC	1525–1375 BC	1375–1050 BC	1050–930 BC

BIBLE BOOKS COVERING EACH PERIOD

Genesis	Genesis Job	Exodus Leviticus Numbers Deuteronomy Joshua	Judges Ruth 1 Samuel	1 & 2 Samuel 1 Kings 1 & 2 Chronicles Psalms Proverbs Ecclesiastes Song of Songs
Adam	Job	**Moses**	Samson	Saul
Eve	**Abraham**	Aaron	Ruth	**David**
Enoch	Isaac	Joshua	Samuel	Solomon
Noah	Jacob			
	Joseph			

Adam & Eve | Canaan → | Abraham | Joshua | Samuel | Saul | David Solomon

Joseph \ Moses
Egypt

WHERE TO FIND THEM

	BOOKS OF LAW	BOOKS OF WISDOM	THE NEW TESTAMENT
	BOOKS OF HISTORY	BOOKS OF PROPHECY	

Period of the Divided Kingdom	The Exile and the Return	Silence Between Old Testament and New Testament	Period of the Life of Christ	The Early Church
930–586 BC	586–400 BC	400 years	5 BC–30 AD	30–100 AD

| 1 & 2 Kings
2 Chronicles
Isaiah-Jeremiah-
Hosea-Joel-Amos-
Ob-Jonah-Micah-
Nahum-Habakkuk-
Zephaniah | Ezra-Nehemiah
Esther
Lamentations
Ezekiel-Daniel
Haggai
Zechariah
Malachi | | Matthew
Mark
Luke
John | Acts-Romans-
1 & 2 Cor-Gal-Eph-
Phil-Col-1 & 2 Thess-
1 & 2 Tim-Titus-Phil-
Heb-James-1 & 2
Peter-1, 2, & 3 John-
Jude-Revelation |

Jeroboam	Ezekiel		Mary	Barnabas
Elijah	Daniel		John the Baptist	**Paul**
Jonah	Esther		**Jesus**	John Mark
Isaiah	Ezra		**Peter**	Luke
Jeremiah	Nehemiah		John	Timothy
			Judas	James

SPLIT Israel/Judah

Fall of Jerusalem 586 BC → Ezra

Babylon

Ascension

By Floyd E Westbrook

SMALL GROUP GUIDE

THE BIBLE COMPANION SERIES ALLOWS members to read and meet at a pace that suits your group. Whether you meet weekly or monthly, the following outline will allow participants to learn from one another's encounters with Scripture. The leader is primarily a facilitator, so it's not necessary that person be a Bible teacher. However, the leader should be familiar with Scripture, willing to direct people to resources when needed, and able to keep the group on track within the agreed-upon schedule.

1. Agree on a meeting schedule: how often, for how long, what day?
2. Agree on a reading pace: not more than six chapters per week is recommended so that the reading load remains manageable.
3. Encourage members to note these reactions:

    - What surprised you?
    - Troubled you?
    - Comforted you?
    - Challenged you?
    - One idea or verse that spoke to you and why.

4. Encourage those who want to go deeper to look up the references and endnotes. Invite them to share what they learn with the group.
5. The opening and closing Scriptures (Psalm 119:18 and benediction) are for participants to say together. The idea is to follow God's example of creating rituals that signal sacred time and build community.

90-MINUTE STUDY GUIDE

Opening

15 minutes   Prayer. "Open my eyes that I may see wonderful things in your law" (Ps. 119:18).

Worship (prayer, music).

Overview

10 minutes   **OPTION 1: BIBLE PROJECT VIDEO**

The Bible Project produces seven-minute overviews of every book of the Bible as well as videos exploring topics and themes found within the books. (Free at bibleproject.com.)

OPTION 2: 5W'S AND H

Using the classic 5W's and an H (Who, What, Where, When, Why, and How), prompt the group to answer these questions about the assigned chapters.

OPTION 3: Leader teaching

Review assigned chapters. Offer insights that highlight one or more themes raised in that week's readings.

Study

45 minutes   Learn from each other

- *Explore* what surprised, troubled, comforted, or challenged you in the assigned readings.
- *Identify* a key verse or idea and consider how it fits into God's bigger story.
- *Discuss* as many COMPANION THOUGHT questions as time allows.

Closing

20 minutes   Prayer for group members and their concerns.

Benediction

Lord . . . I know that you can do all things; no purpose of yours can be thwarted.

JOB 42:2

ENDNOTES

1 Tremper Longman III, "Israelite Genres in Their Ancient Near Eastern Context" from *The Changing Face of Form Criticism for the Twenty-First Century* (Grand Rapids, MI: William B. Eerdmans Publishing Company, 2003), 178.

2 H. Dubrow uses a similar example in her book on genre. *Genre: The Critical Idiom*; (New York: Methuen, 1982), 1–3.

3 Tremper Longman III, *How to Read the Psalms,* How to Read Series (Downers Grove, IL: InterVarsity Press, 1988), 22.

4 Poetry makes up a large portion of the Old Testament. Tremper Longman III, *How to Read the Psalms*, in the How to Read Series (Downers Grove, IL: InterVarsity Press, 1988), 90–91. Some scholars estimate as much of a third of the Old Testament is poetry. See '"How Should Poetry in the Bible be Interpreted?" Got Questions Ministries, https://www.gotquestions.org/poetry-in-the-Bible.html.≠

5 Moses and Mariam lead the Israelites in a sung poem in Exodus 15. Hannah's prayer in 1 Samuel 2 and Mary's song in Luke 1:46–55 are poems. The book of Lamentation, mourning the demise of Jerusalem, is entirely poetry. In Revelation, poetry breaks through the devastation of the end times to celebrate that God is in control (Rev. 5:9–10, 13; 7:12; 11:17–18; 15:3–4; 16:5–6).

6 Longman, *How to Read the Psalms*, 90–91.

7 Kenneth Barker, Mark L. Strauss, Jeannine K. Brown, Craig L. Bloomberg, and Michael Williams, introduction to Job notes, *The NIV Study Bible Notes, Fully Revised Edition* (Grand Rapids, MI: Zondervan, 2020), Kindle edition.

8 There is no definitive evidence of wisdom schools per se in Babylonian culture, but debates between disciples of various teachers were common. John H. Walton, Victor H. Matthews, and Mark W. Chavalas, Proverbs 1:1–9:18 notes, *The IVP Bible Background Commentary: Old Testament*, in the IVP Bible Background Commentary Set, IVP Academic (Downers Grove, Illinois), Kindle edition.

9 Belief in one God who is all powerful and wise was unique in the polytheistic culture of the ancient world. John H. Walton and Tremper Longman III, *How to Read Job*, in the How to Read Series (Downers Grove, IL: InterVarsity Press, 2020), Kindle edition, 30.

10 Robert Alter maintains that if such schools existed, the author of Job is not a product of one but a rogue writer, dissenting from the perspective taught by such schools. Robert Alter, *The Wisdom Books: Job, Proverbs, and Ecclesiastes: A Translation with Commentary* (New York: W. W. Norton & Company, 2010), Kindle edition, 20.

11 Walton and Longman, *How to Read Job*, 87.

12 Walton and Longman, *How to Read Job*, 89.

13 Romans 11:35 quotes Job 41:11, and 1 Corinthians 3:19 quotes Job 5:13.

14 Bible scholar Dr. Russel P. Spittler coined the word "deologue" as an alternative to "theologue." (A theological student is a theologue.) Here, "deologue" (taken from *deus*, the Greek word for God) indicates a divine discourse.

15 *NIV Study Bible* notes, Job 4:1.

16 Joseph becomes prime minister of Egypt and saves God's people from starvation (Gen. 41:41–43). Esther becomes queen of Persia and saves God's people from genocide (Esther 7–8). Ruth becomes the grandmother of King David, from whose line Jesus comes (Ruth 4:17).

17 The principle that wisdom is saying (or doing) the right thing at the right time to the right person is pointedly taught in the wisdom books (Job, Psalms, Proverbs, Ecclesiastes, Song of Songs). See Walton and Longman, *How to Read Job*, chapter 12. Also Tremper Longman III, *How to Read Proverbs*, in the How to Read Series (Downers Grove, IL: InterVarsity Press, 2002), 14–15.

18 In the ancient world, hades (Greek) and Sheol (Hebrew) were names for the underworld, a place where all people were thought to go after death. In time hades became associated with the idea of eternal punishment and our idea of hell. For a deeper discussion, see Richard Bauckham, "Hades, Hell," *The Anchor Yale Bible Dictionary*, ed. David Noel Freedman (New York: Doubleday, 1992), 14.

19 N. T. Parker and Amy L. Balogh, "Redeemer," *The Lexham Bible Dictionary*, ed. John D. Barry et al., (Bellingham, WA: Lexham Press, 2016).

20 Revelation 20 describes two judgments. One determines whether we have the right to enter God's presence, and the other holds us accountable for our deeds. Hebrews 9:27 says, "People are destined to die once, and after that to face judgment." When that day comes, several books are opened. Some hold us accountable for what we have done, but the Book of Life determines our destiny. This book holds the name of every person whose sins have been forgiven through faith in Jesus Christ.

21 Malachi 3:18 says that on Judgment Day "'you will again see the distinction between the righteous and the wicked, between those who serve God and those who do not.'"

22 Proverbs 8:22–31 says wisdom existed before time. Wisdom was present at creation. The New Testament reveals that wisdom is found in the person of Jesus Christ (1 Cor. 1:24, 30).

23 For a deeper look at how God's wisdom may be evident in a nonbeliever, see Karen Westbrook Moderow, *The Bible Companion Book 7 Proverbs–Song of Songs* (Dana Point, CA: Jordanwest Publications, 2024), Proverbs 22D

24 We are told what behaviors and attitudes please God throughout the Old and New Testaments. For an overview, see Exodus 20:1–17, Proverbs 5, and Matthew 5:17–19.

25 A. R. Millard, "Sages, Schools, Education," *Dictionary of the Old Testament: Wisdom, Poetry & Writings*, ed. Tremper Longman III and Peter Enns (Downers Grove, IL; Nottingham, England: IVP Academic; Inter-Varsity Press, 2008), 708.

26 Proverbs 8:12–31 says wisdom existed before time. Wisdom was present at creation. The New Testament reveals that wisdom is found in the person of Jesus Christ (1 Cor. 1:24, 30).

27 Many Psalms and New Testament Scriptures refute the idea that God views hurting people as wicked and won't help them. The Father sent Jesus to save us, proving the opposite. Verses such as Psalm 34:17–18, 1 Timothy 1:15, Romans 5:8, and Mark 2:17 assure us that God does listen to the cries of the oppressed.

28 Elijah, Ezekiel, and the disciples also encounter God in a life-changing way during or after storms (1 Kings 19:11–13; Ezek.1:4; Matt. 8:23–27).

ACKNOWLEDGMENTS

To my husband, Joe, and my sons, Michael and David—thank you for your love and unwavering belief in me. Your generous gifts of time and freedom made it possible for me to write this series. I love you to the moon and back.

My dear family and friends, your prayers, encouragement, and wisdom have guided me throughout my publishing journey. I am forever grateful.

To my editorial team—Christina Miller, Dori Harrell, Amanda Blake, Colleen Jones, Ray Dittmeier, Jonathan Lewis, and David Moderow—your diligence, talents, and passion brought this project to life. Thank you, thank you!

ORDER INFORMATION

JORDANWEST

To order additional copies of this book, please visit
www.thebiblecompanionseries.com
or www.karenwestbrookmoderow.com

Charts created for this series may be downloaded from
The Bible Companion website:
www.thebiblecompanionseries.com

Made in the USA
Columbia, SC
19 August 2025